© Aladdin Books 1991

First published in 1992
in the United States by
Gloucester Press Inc.
95 Madison Avenue
New York, NY 10016

Library of Congress Cataloging-in-Publication Data

Hodge, Anthony.
    Cartooning / by Anthony Hodge.
       p.   cm. -- (Hands on arts and crafts)
    Includes index.
    Summary: Uses a series of simple projects to
provide a step-by-step introduction to a range of
cartooning techniques.
    ISBN 0-531-17322-4 (lib. bdg.)
    1. Cartooning--Technique--Juvenile literature.
[1. Cartooning--Technique. 2. Drawing-
-Technique.] I. Title. II. Series: Hodge, Anthony.
Hands on arts and crafts.
NC1320.H527   1992
741.5--dc20   91-34409   CIP   AC

Printed in Belgium

The author, Anthony Hodge, is an artist whose work is
regularly exhibited. He has taught art to adults and
children for 20 years.

Design: Rob Hillier and Andy Wilkinson
Editor: Jen Green
Drawings by Anthony Hodge
Illustrations by Ron Hayward Associates

HANDS ON ARTS AND CRAFTS

CARTOONING

Anthony Hodge

Gloucester Press
London · New York · Toronto · Sydney

CONTENTS

INTRODUCTION

Cartooning is about having fun and developing a new skill at the same time. If you are the sort of person who sees the funny side of things, now is the chance to get some of your ideas down on paper. And if you've always wanted to have adventures, now you can invent strip cartoons in which anything can happen.

This book introduces you to different kinds of cartoons and to the wide range of materials you can use for cartooning. You don't need to be great at drawing; many cartoons are based on a few simple lines.

The first cartoons

Originally a cartoon was a sketch made in preparation for a more finished work – an outline for a painting, tapestry, or mosaic. The cartoons made by the Italian artist Leonardo da Vinci in the fifteenth century are still famous today. Today, a cartoon is a particular kind of drawing, direct and effective, often funny. The best cartoons often say something about life that everyone knows deep down to be true, but is afraid to own up to! A sequence of cartoons may be used to tell a story – a comic strip – or they can be used to make a cartoon film.

▷ *"These four cartoons are of characters who just emerged when I started doodling. There's no limit to the number and variety of types waiting to jump out of your head too. The one at the top right thinks he is drawing something very funny – I hope this happens to you!"*

JOKES AND CARICATURES

Over the next pages you can see the different types of cartoon and the materials they can be drawn with.

Visual jokes

The simplest cartoon of all is a picture which makes a joke. The drawing itself can also be funny, or can surprise us. Alternatively, it's the cartoon character who's about to get a surprise; we can see it coming but the character can't!

Some cartoon jokes are effective without words; others rely on a worded caption to make the point. If more than one character is speaking, speech bubbles will be needed.

Pencil and felt-tip pen

The most basic tools for cartooning are pencils and felt-tips. A soft pencil produces a friendly line (below left). You can go over a sketch in pencil with felt-tip or ink, and then rub out mistakes with an eraser.

Felt-tips come in different thicknesses. A fine pen makes an elegant line (center) and a thick or chiseled marker (right) produces strong, solid marks.

Many kinds of paper are suitable for cartooning. Newsprint paper is inexpensive. Thin paper like tracing paper is useful for tracing and redoing images if you make a mistake.

Caricature

A caricature is a drawing of a real person in which individual features, like the size of the person's nose, or the shape of the chin, are exaggerated. Yet, somehow a likeness is achieved. In fact, if cleverly done, a caricature can look more like the individual than he or she does in real life! Some people, unfortunately for them, are easier to caricature than others.

This style of cartooning has a long history. For thousands of years cartoonists have been making caricatures of public figures. They can be kind or cruel, flattering or grotesque, depending on the artist.

Ink, charcoal and conté

Pen and ink, charcoal and conté are all lively materials suitable for caricaturing different kinds of people. Ink can be used with a dip-pen or a fountain pen, and with nibs of different sizes. Ink makes free, expressive lines (left below).

Charcoal gives a dark line for dramatic portraits (middle below). It can produce a rough and ready look, or can be smudged with your finger to make velvety shadows.

Conté comes in shades of brown or gray. It produces soft, warm marks good for caricatures like the hairy, bearlike person below right.

CARTOON STRIPS AND ANIMATION

Cartoon strips

Cartoon strips are a sequence of individual cartoons that tell a story. From cave paintings to the Bayeux tapestry, from Mickey Mouse to Superman, the principle is to show developing action through a series of images. Have a look through some of your own cartoon books to see the vast range of styles that can be used.

We often enjoy strip cartoons without noticing the techniques artists use to show closeup or long distance views, to indicate drama, tension, or a change of pace. Filmmakers and animators use similar techniques to produce the same kinds of effects.

Cartooning in color

Cartoon strips are usually in color. Many color materials are available. Colored pencils are easy to use. You can create pale and dark tones by pressing lightly or heavily, and new colors by laying one color over another (left). Watercolor and gouache (middle picture) are both good for cartooning. Watercolor is washed on thinly and is transparent. Gouache is denser and opaque. For both you will need to use thick paper, as thin paper will wrinkle up.

Felt-tips (right) are also versatile. Chunky, wedge-shaped ones cover the paper quickly and evenly; thin ones are good for outlines.

Animation

Animation is a way of bringing pictures to life by making them appear to move. When we watch a modern cartoon film, we seem to see a smooth sequence of movement. It's hard to believe we are actually looking at thousands of single pictures, each one slightly different from the last. They change in front of our eyes so quickly we can't see when one image replaces another.

Later in the book we will look at the techniques animators use. You can practice some of these tricks yourself. If you enjoy being precise and working carefully, you can get some very impressive results.

Painting on acetate

For the purposes of animation, cartoons are painted on sheets of clear plastic called acetate. Both sides of the acetate are used, as shown below. The image is drawn on one side with a special oil-based pen called an o.h.p. (overhead projector pen). The image is colored in on the other side using gouache or acrylic paint. This may be done quite messily, because when the acetate is turned over again, the brush marks will be invisible. Small pads of acetate are available and can be bought in art stores. Try cartooning on acetate yourself; the result will look very effective positioned on a window with light shining through it.

BASICS: HEADS GALORE

All styles of cartooning rely on a few basic ideas. Let's look at them first in terms of cartooning heads.

Faces are everywhere if you know how to look, in trees and clouds, even in clothes hanging on the door knob at night. For the cartoonist, using the imagination is very important.

Eggheads

A cartoon head usually starts life as a balloon or egg shape. The basic ingredients of a face are two dots for eyes, an L-shape for a nose and a line for the mouth. But the way you combine these basic ingredients can suggest all kinds of characters (see the faces below left).

Begin your cartooning career by doing variations on this theme. Then experiment with different shapes, choosing a particular shape for the head and echoing the same shape as you draw in the features.

Positioning the features
Eyes set far apart look confident; eyes set close together (bottom right) look silly, or shy. Features placed at the bottom of the head look clever; features placed at the top look self-satisfied.

Shapes and personalities
The shape of the head suggests personality; draw features to match. A pear-shaped face looks sad, a square head looks mechanical. A curvy face looks flabby and a star-shape is full of energy.

Faces step by step

Try building your own cartoon personalities. Start with a basic head shape and gradually add features, hair and clothes. Then draw your character again, with a different expression this time.

▽ *"Expressions affect not only the mouth but all the features, the shape of the face, even the hair. Try some expressions yourself in front of the mirror. Cartoon expressions are even more pronounced."*

BASICS: GETTING THINGS MOVING

Action in cartoons needs to be shown as simply and clearly as possible. The secret of drawing cartoon figures on the move is to start with a few simple lines and build up from there.

The skeleton is the basis of all figures, human or animal; that's where stick people come in. The stick figure represents the skeleton and is an ideal way of practicing positions and movements. Try a series of stick figures before you commit yourself to a more developed drawing.

▷ *"Action can often be summed up by a single line. One way to get your imagination moving is to sketch a line at random and see what it can be turned into! The examples on the right show lines of movement evolving into finished cartoons. Notice how movement can be emphasized by the addition of speed lines and small details like the flying pipe and hat."*

▽ *"Fill pages of your sketch book with stick people running, jumping, somersaulting, doing everything under the sun! When you're happy with your action people, start to flesh them out into sausage figures, as shown below."*

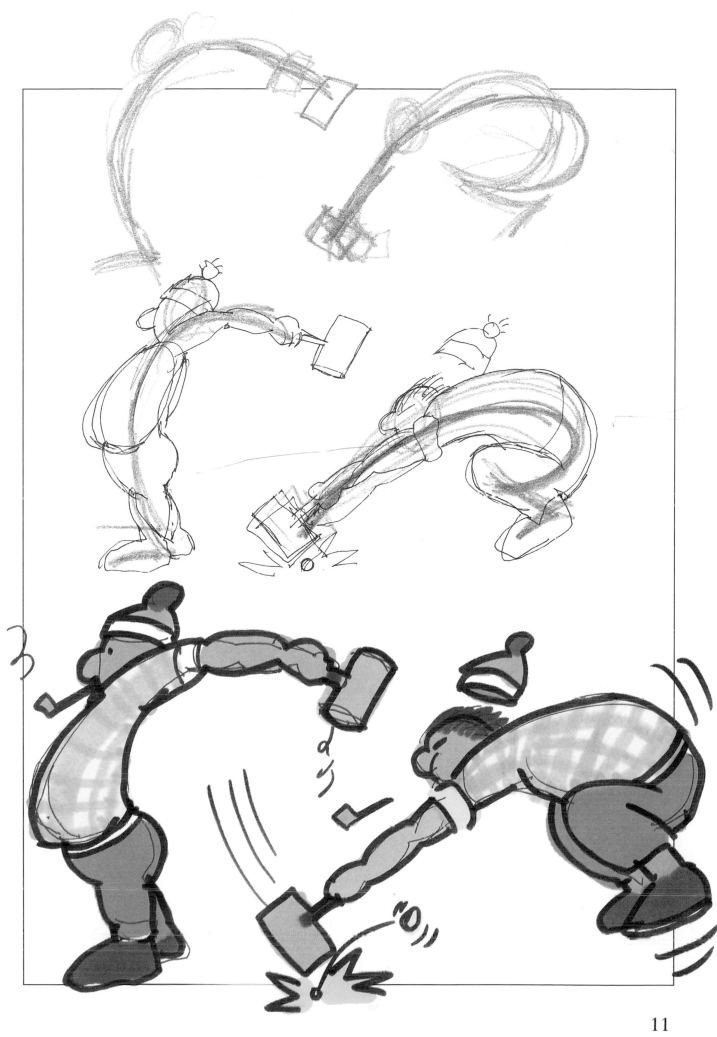

BASICS: POINTS OF VIEW

"Everybody's got to be somewhere," as a comedian once said. Where are you now? Everyone reading this will give a different answer. In cartoons the action can be set anywhere from the bottom of the sea to the inside of a shoe. Sometimes the best jokes have more to do with the setting than what the characters are doing or saying.

How things change size

Cartoon backgrounds are usually kept simple. But in cartoons, as in real life, things look bigger the closer they are to you, and things look small if they are far away. This is called perspective, and in cartoons the effect is often even more exaggerated. Look at the girl on the railroad track (bottom left below). The train is really bigger than she is but it seems smaller because it's further away.

Looking up and down

Perspective affects how things appear from different angles, as you can see from the cartoons on the right. The same knight looks very different from various angles: straight on, from below and above. Parts of his body loom large, or dwindle away, depending on how close they are to us. It takes a bit of practice to get this looking right, and it may help to work from stick and sausage men, as you did on the previous page.

▷ *"Different angles increase the drama and impact of your cartooning. The face-on view is the least dramatic. Seen from below looking up (not a good idea in this instance) the knight's feet and fists look huge. Viewed from above, his helmet and sword seem to zoom toward us as he sweeps past."*

Tiny or tremendous?

Background makes all the difference to how we understand, or "read," a cartoon. The top two cartoons on the left show how the same girl seems to change size, depending on the background she is seen against. Playing with scale is fun and there are lots of tricks you can try. Practice putting your own character in different settings.

Putting things in perspective

The girl on the railroad track is an example of a kind of perspective called linear, or line, perspective.

The lines of the railroad track run parallel. But they appear to converge and meet at a point on the horizon called the vanishing point. All parallel lines obey this rule. Sketching lines in pencil fanning in toward the vanishing point (see the drawings above) can help get things in perspective.

Perspective can also be shown by a technique called overlapping. The girl overlaps and conceals some of the houses (bottom right) and so seems to be standing in front of them. The car overlaps the sidewalk and so looks the closest of all.

CARTOON PUNS

At its simplest a cartoon is something that makes us laugh. What kinds of things do *you* find funny? It's a great feeling when something you thought of makes other people laugh too. On this page we will look at the most basic jokes of all, those without words or captions, and explore how you can dream them up for yourself.

Visual puns

Many jokes without words rely on visual puns. A visual pun is a joke based on a shape with two meanings, just as a verbal pun is based on a word with two meanings. The cartoon at the top on the opposite page is an example of a visual pun.

Doodle power

Develop your ability to find visual puns by doodling. Draw a simple shape, like the rectangle, coil and zig-zag patterns shown in red below. Or draw some random squiggles with a friend and then swap over. Have a good look at the lines and see what they suggest to you. Turn the paper around and look at it from all sides. Your squiggle could be anything – it's a question of allowing your imagination to run wild.

Variations on a zig-zag

Below are some ideas for visual puns based on a zig-zag line. It's important not to think or try too hard; just doodle and see what happens. Try the same exercise with other shapes, like the ones shown on the left.

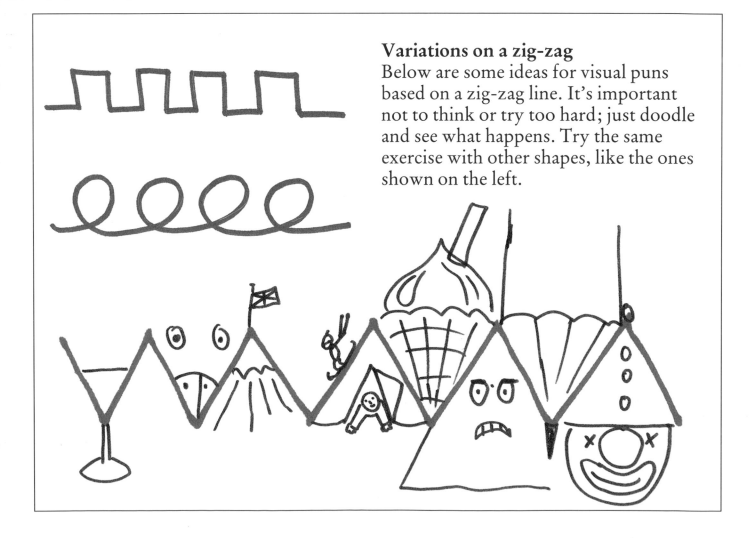

Doing two jobs

Another type of joke without words is about an object with two functions. The blindfold is common to both pictures below, but in the second it is put to an unexpected use. What other everyday objects can you think of that could have more than one use? Let your imagination loose on objects like umbrellas, baby carriages, aerosol sprays and walking sticks.

▷ *"This visual pun is drawn from the doodle on the previous page. The humor in many cartoons is based on anticipation: something is about to happen, but the character involved is not aware of it – yet!"*

Getting your point across

The joke here is about the blindfold, so it has been colored black to make it obvious. All the details in the first picture – the guns, the expressions of soldiers and prisoner – lead us to expect the worst. In the second picture the details reappear but are changed, emphasizing the contrast in mood.

I SUPPOSE YOU FIND THAT FUNNY

Some people think cartoons without words are the best. But whether in the form of speech bubbles, captions or signs, words add a whole new range of possibilities. Thinking up jokes is easier for some of us than for others. Exercises with words encourage jokes to spring to mind.

The punch line game

In cartoon jokes the point is often put across in the caption below the picture, called the punch line. An exercise you can try involves a simple punch line like "I suppose you find that funny." The exercise is to think of as many ways as possible to illustrate it. At least two people are implied, one of whom is not amused by the antics of the other. But what is happening, exactly?

There are other punch lines you could try with this. Possibilities include "Don't look now, but...," "I thought you said there were no side effects," or even "We can't go on meeting like this." Sketch rough ideas and develop one or two.

Do you read me?

In cartoon speech, words themselves are only part of the message. The shape you write in and the lettering you use can help get the message across.

Speech usually appears within a round bubble, but a speech box with straight lines can suggest tough or fierce words. Thought clouds tell you what's in a character's mind, and whispers usually appear within radiating lines.

Pow!

Loud noise is expressed in large colored letters. Both the style of lettering and the shape in which the word appears increase the effect. A starshape implies an impact or explosion. Letters can be overlapped to create a three-dimensional look, and to suggest movement and speed.

Whatever style you use, words must be legible. Rule lines for your words in pencil, and write evenly in capitals.

Lost in the jungle or all at sea?
Cartoonists often return to classic comic situations like hospitals, prisons, or car accidents. Why are these situations funny? They are often dangerous, embarrassing or unexpected – situations we'd rather not be in ourselves!

The joke is usually about how ordinary people react to extraordinary circumstances. Someone carried off by a monster might, for example, worry about whether they locked the back door. Funny things happen in everyday life too. Jot down ideas in a notebook for later use.

Shipwrecked? Stranded on the moon?
Below are two of the most common dilemmas cartoon characters find themselves in. Practice the punch line game in reverse by thinking up as many punch lines as possible for these two images. Bear in mind all the possible interpretations of the pictures.

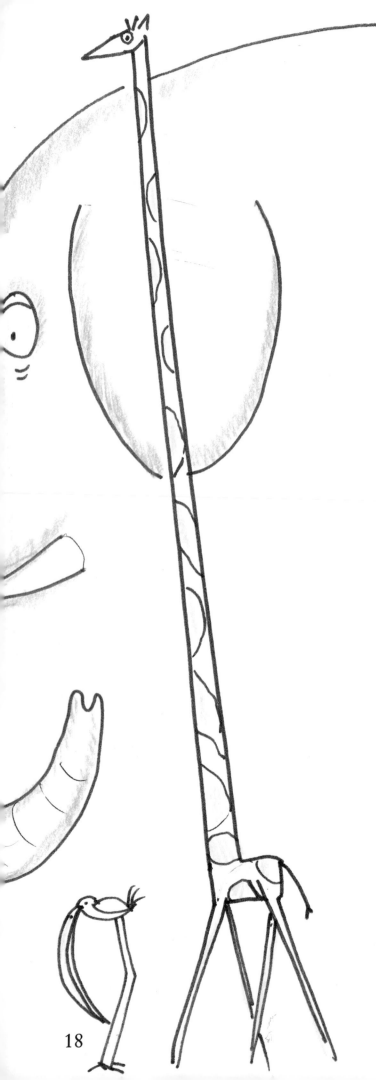

CARICATURE

Have you got a nickname? If you haven't, your teacher probably has. Nicknames are a bit like shorthand; we use them to sum people up, not always very kindly. If they stick, it's usually because they pinpoint something about that person's appearance or personality.

Caricatures are visual nicknames. Like nicknames, they focus on certain key characteristics and emphasize them. Like other kinds of cartoons, they are about simplifying and exaggerating what you see.

Animal crackers

Some caricaturists say that it helps them to think of a person as a particular animal. When we draw animals from imagination, we tend to focus on their most obvious features and emphasize them. A grizzly bear is all shaggy hair; a rhino is built like a tank, with stumpy legs and a giant horn. A monkey is thin and gangling, with rubbery legs and tail. Try caricaturing animals yourself from imagination or from photographs. Try doing a realistic drawing of each animal first, and then exaggerate it into a caricature.

◁ *"The main thing about an elephant is size. To emphasize this I've made mine so big it can't fit on the page, but I've left enough clues to identify it. Of course, the first thing you notice about a giraffe is the long neck. Wading birds have long legs and curved beaks for picking things off the bottom of the river bed, so these are the things I've chosen to exaggerate."*

Stretching a point

The same idea holds true of caricaturing both people and animals. Whether you choose your "victim" from real life or from photographs, you will need to get to know their face well. Study the face and decide which features – eyes, chin, hair, whatever – are most important. Make these stand out even more.

Not just heads

What you choose to emphasize is up to you. Two cartoonists will produce very different caricatures of the same person. And remember that caricatures can be about bodies, too. The size of chest or stomach, the length of arms and legs, the posture, whether slouched or upright, can all help your caricature work.

What's in a face?

In caricature the trick is to sum up and exaggerate. The first caricature below has focussed on the boy's frizzy hair and cheeky grin; the second (top right) has made the most of the eyeglasses, pointed nose and glum mouth of its subject. The studious girl gets messier hair, a snub nose and a more fixed expression, and the young man (bottom right) has an even haughtier look.

19

DO-IT-YOURSELF CARICATURE

Now that you know how caricature works, it's time to try some of your own. The first step is to choose your subject. It's good to pick someone you know well, and who you can observe from day to day. But you could try doing a caricature of a famous person you admire, or even one whom you dislike!

That's typical!

Before you begin drawing, you may have to do a bit of creative thinking.

Consider what pose, and what habits are most typical of your subject. Capturing the essence of someone's personality need not involve drawing their face or even much of their body at all. If Grandad spends most of his time in an armchair reading the newspaper, you could draw the newspaper with two hands holding it open and just the top of his head surrounded by the chair. Add smoke from a pipe and his old red slippers and it couldn't be anyone else.

The right tool for the job

Make sure the drawing materials you choose match your subject. Remember that pencils, pen and ink, charcoal, and conté all have a very different "feel."

Charcoal (below left) has a rich, soft look. Pen and ink has a spontaneous quality. The caricature on the right uses an ink wash to create shadows and a depressed, seedy look.

20

Clothes always help to identify your subject. Some people's hats and coats are so particular to them that a back view may be enough. Some people like to hide behind their accessories – look at the charcoal portrait far left on the opposite page.

▽ *"Caricatures of famous people can be fun: I chose John Wayne (below). First I did a drawing from a photograph to familiarize myself with my subject. I noted a square chin, the lift of one eyebrow. From movies I remembered a habit of talking out of one side of his mouth. As John Wayne is best known for cowboy parts, I added a hat, kerchief and checked shirt."*

CREATING A SUPERHERO

A cartoon strip is a series of pictures that tell a story, from the adventures of mischievous school friends to the exploits of fantasy superheroes. The next two pages are about creating your own cartoon strip, and the first step is to invent the characters.

What do Superman, the Incredible Hulk and the Teenage Mutant Ninja Turtles have in common? Most superheroes are concocted from a recipe of certain ingredients. Looking at these ingredients can help you build your own characters.

Factor X
Some superheroes come from other planets but most are from Earth; they are ordinary people (or animals) who have acquired a special ability, often as a result of some extraordinary event. This is sometimes linked to radiation, but not always; Popeye gets his great strength from an ordinary can of spinach.

A superhero has his or her own territory, a particular location to patrol. Cities are popular, and, of course, the far reaches of outer space.

Missions and superskills
All superheroes have a cause – to fight villains like the one shown above left, or to right a particular injustice in the world. Your superhero will need a mission and a special ability – think about the superpower you would most like to have for yourself!

A superpower can be extra strength, vision, or hearing, or it can be something new, from X ray vision to the ability to change shape. A superhero associated with an animal takes on the creature's powers – so the owl girl above might be able to see in the dark. Other favorite crime-fighters are themselves animals.

Developing a script

Your superhero can be developed by thinking about costume, weaknesses, likes and dislikes, sidekicks and friends. But the best way of learning about your superhero is to set out on an adventure and see how he or she performs!

What makes a good storyline? Cartoon scripts often contain certain key ingredients. The strip begins with a problem: a crime or mystery which is often the work of a villain. It may be almost too late before the hero learns of the trouble and decides to step in.

Meanwhile, problems may mount up, and friends may be captured or wounded. In the nick of time comes a moment of inspiration, and the tide turns. Triumph! There is often a celebration before the hero heads home. Develop your plot along these lines and your superhero is ready to go!

▷ *"My superhero, Cartoonman, is a cool customer; here you can see him studying his script, unconcerned by the battle raging around him. To find out what problems lie in store for him, see the script in the box above."*

Cartoonman's first adventure Rocketwoman is guiding her spaceship across the galaxy when the engine develops a fault. Forced to crash land on an unknown planet, she is besieged by alien lifeforms. Using his superhearing, Cartoonman learns of the danger. He speeds to the planet and soon has things sorted out. Returning Rocketwoman to her own planet, he receives a hero's send off and returns to base.

YOUR OWN CARTOON STRIP

When you've invented your superhero and developed a script, it's time to plan how to illustrate the action. In the best cartoon strips, the reader follows the plot, and also enjoys the strip as a visual adventure. Varying the size and shape of your pictures, or *frames*, changing the scale and perspective, all add to the impact of your tale.

A story in a single page
Sketch out some rough designs or *layouts* for your story. You only need to illustrate the main points, and leave the rest for the reader to imagine. Different frame sizes will be appropriate for showing key moments of action and for conveying necessary information.

Color is important. Different characters and locations should have different colors so that the reader can recognize them at a glance. Use strong colors for foregrounds, quieter colors for backgrounds.

When you're happy with your layout, fill in your frames, perhaps working in pencil at first and finishing off in ink and in color.

▷ **"Cartoonman's first adventure is illustrated on the opposite page. But you'll see I've used the speech bubbles to include some more tips on page layout. Can you imagine the actual words the characters would have used?"**

Laying out your page
Below are three sample page layouts. Try to see your page of cartoons as a single picture made up of different elements. Using only a small number of colors will help with this.

As these examples illustrate, cartoon frames don't have to be rectangular. Some images will fit better into a different shape. A diagonal line leads the eye on to the next frame; ovals and circles liven up the page. Experiment with your own alternatives, tracing round objects to get circles and curves.

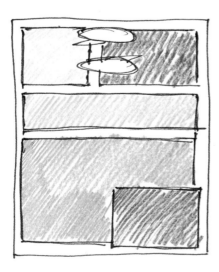  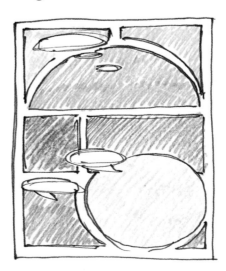

FLICK BOOK ANIMATION

The art of making pictures move is called animation. This need not be technical – it can be as easy and effective as the projects here.

Making a two-page flick book
The simplest form of animation is the flick book (below). All you need to make this is a pencil and a long strip of paper about three inches wide. The paper should be thin enough to see through, but should not be too fragile. Fold the strip in half, crease it and open it out again.

Before and after
Think of an action or event you want to illustrate, involving "before" and "after" positions. Draw the first stage of your idea on the second page of the two-page "book." In the example below, this is the man with smooth hair. Fold the first page of the book back over the image. You should be able to make out something of the picture underneath.

For your flick book to be effective, some parts of your image should remain the same. Trace these through the paper, then draw in the different parts that will appear to move.

Trial run
Once you've drawn your second picture, roll it up tightly around a pencil. Hold the paper down as shown at the bottom below. Then run your pencil left and right, to reveal your "before" and "after" pictures alternately.

Sample flick books
Below are two other "before" and "after" ideas. How about before and after going on vacation, using a hair restorer or taking a weight-loss pill?

Animated notebooks

Now try a further sequence of action. You'll need a notebook with blank pages of thin paper. Think of an action, and decide how many stages you need to illustrate it – the example shown uses nine.

Draw the key stages in your note book first, pages 1, 5, and 9 shown here, starting on page 9 with the last in the sequence. Trace the unmoving parts of the picture through the paper. Then fill in the pictures in between, again working from the back of the book.

▷ *"When all your stages are complete, flick the pages of your notebook and watch your picture come to life! The more accurate your tracing is, the more effective this will be."*

MOVING PICTURES

If you had the power to slow life down, you might see all movement as a series of tiny changes. The project here is about seeing complex action in this way. It will help to develop the skill of seeing as an animator does – in slow motion, one step at a time.

In your mind's eye

Think of a sequence of action like the one below, involving your superhero perhaps. As in the second flick book project, you will need to concentrate on the key moments of action first. These are your *key frames*, the beginning and end of the movement, and two or three other stages that sum up what is going on.

Once you're happy with your key frames, you'll need to sketch in the action in between (in pencil in the illustration below). These stages are known as "in-betweeners." You can choose to use tracing paper to reproduce the parts of your drawing that remain the same, and even the parts that look the same but have been moved to a different position.

Key frames and in-betweeners

In the cartoon industry, teams of illustrators are employed to produce action sequences. Artists working on full-length cartoon films use the system of key frames and in-betweeners. Only the key frames are drawn by an animator, leaving an artist, also called an "in-betweener," to fill in all the others.

▽ *"Not too easy for you and me, perhaps, but anything is possible in the world of animation. The four key frames are shown in color, and the in-betweeners are inserted to complete the sequence."*

Using a light box

Professional animators draw on sheets of transparent plastic called acetate. For tracing the parts of the image which remain the same in the next frame, animators use a light box (below). The completed sheet is pegged in position. A second sheet is laid on top. When the light box is switched on, the first image can be seen clearly, and parts of it traced.

Animation

Have you any idea how many separate pictures are needed for a full-length cartoon film? Hundreds? Thousands, perhaps? In fact, it's nearly a million. All this work used to be done by hand. Today, some of it can be done by computers.

Once a cartoon image is finished, it is photographed individually and becomes one frame of the film. There are 24 of these frames in one second of film time. When the film is shown in a theater, the frames change so fast that what we see is nonstop action.

▽ *"An animator uses a light box to see the outlines of a cartoon more clearly."*

29

CARTOON PROJECTS

Some of the techniques explored in this book can be used to make presents for your family and friends.

Your own comic
Aim high by publishing your own comic book. Include all your best jokes, and the exploits of your cartoon strip heroes. Invent adventures with plots to be continued in the next issue; your friends will soon be clamoring for the next edition. Why not combine efforts with a friend or two? You could even try drawing a cartoon strip with a friend, doing alternate pictures and making it up as you go along.

Cartoon cards
Many of your drawings will make great cards. Your best two-frame joke, with the first picture on the front and the punch line inside, will work well.

Caricature cards are another possibility, but be careful who you send them to! On the left you can see someone receiving a caricature birthday card with mixed feelings.

Your favorite flick books can also make excellent cards. You could even include a pencil and instructions. The front page of your flick book must be on thin paper, or it won't roll around the pencil. For the other cards you could choose to work on thicker paper or cardboard, so that your finished product will stand up. Or you can cut out your cartoons and stick them onto cardboard with glue.

PRACTICAL TIPS

Protecting your equipment
Keeping your drawing equipment safe is important. Store your paper, pencils and drawing pads together in one place. This will help from a practical point of view, and give you a feeling of continuity in your work. Protect your paper by storing it away in a drawer where it can lie flat and will not get creased or soiled when it is not being used.

Getting rid of mistakes
Even professional cartoonists make mistakes. Erasers, of course, take care of errors in pencil. If your drawing is in a more permanent medium like felt-tip, tracing is a good way of saving the parts you're happy with. Thin paper like typing paper is easy to see through and trace with. Hold other kinds of paper against the window to see the drawing beneath.

Tracing is slow and careful work, and can inhibit you if your style is free and spontaneous. Your art store will stock small pots of opaque white watercolor which you can use to paint out any errors. New lines can be drawn in over the top.

Alternatively, you could cut a fresh piece of paper to cover your mistake and paste it over the top with glue. Mistakes on acetate can be sponged off with water.

Working with felt-tips
Felt-tips are excellent color tools. Use them to fill in areas of paper quickly and evenly. When you finish using a color, it's important to put the cap back on, or it will have dried out by the next time you need it! Remember that felt-tips soak through thin paper, so don't have anything precious underneath.

Stick mostly to light colors, and use strong ones mainly for detail. To some extent, felt-tips can be laid down over one another to create new colors. When not blending colors, allow time for one color to dry before applying another next to it, otherwise your work may smudge.

Fixative
If you're working with charcoal or conté, you will need to seal your work with fixative to prevent it from smudging. Cans are available from art stores. Place your finished drawing in a well-ventilated area and spray fixative back and forth over it. Be careful not to get any in your eyes.

The dictionary game
Coming up with ideas for cartoons, particularly for cartoon jokes, is easier for some of us than others. One exercise which can encourage the flow of ideas is the dictionary game. Get a dictionary and pick two words from it at random. Think up a way of linking them in a picture. If nothing springs to mind, try another word, but don't cheat too much!

INDEX

▽ *"His mission accomplished, our hero flies off into a cartoon sunset. This picture was sketched in pencil and finished in felt-tip."*

PRINTED IN BELGIUM BY

proost
INTERNATIONAL BOOK PRODUCTION